**Facts About the Grey Squirrel**

**By Lisa Strattin**

**© 2016 Lisa Strattin**

**Revised 2022 © Lisa Strattin**

# FREE BOOK

## FREE FOR ALL SUBSCRIBERS

LisaStrattin.com/Subscribe-Here

# BOX SET

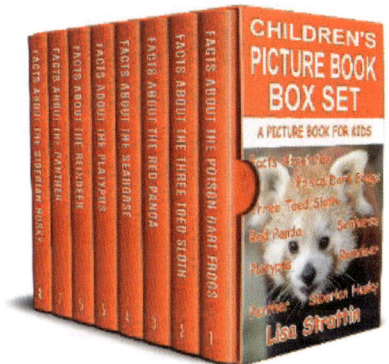

- **FACTS ABOUT THE POISON DART FROGS**
- **FACTS ABOUT THE THREE TOED SLOTH**
  - **FACTS ABOUT THE RED PANDA**
  - **FACTS ABOUT THE SEAHORSE**
  - **FACTS ABOUT THE PLATYPUS**
  - **FACTS ABOUT THE REINDEER**
  - **FACTS ABOUT THE PANTHER**
- **FACTS ABOUT THE SIBERIAN HUSKY**

## LisaStrattin.com/BookBundle

**Facts for Kids Picture Books by Lisa Strattin**

Little Blue Penguin, Vol 92

Chipmunk, Vol 5

Frilled Lizard, Vol 39

Blue and Gold Macaw, Vol 13

Poison Dart Frogs, Vol 50

Blue Tarantula, Vol 115

African Elephants, Vol 8

Amur Leopard, Vol 89

Sabre Tooth Tiger, Vol 167

Baboon, Vol 174

Sign Up for New Release Emails Here

LisaStrattin.com/subscribe-here

All rights reserved. No part of this book may be reproduced by any means whatsoever without the written permission from the author, except brief portions quoted for purpose of review.

All information in this book has been carefully researched and checked for factual accuracy. However, the author and publisher makes no warranty, express or implied, that the information contained herein is appropriate for every individual, situation or purpose and assume no responsibility for errors or omissions. The reader assumes the risk and full responsibility for all actions, and the author will not be held responsible for any loss or damage, whether consequential, incidental, special or otherwise, that may result from the information presented in this book.

All images are free for use or purchased from stock photo sites or royalty free for commercial use.

Some coloring pages might be of the general species due to lack of available images.

I have relied on my own observations as well as many different sources for this book and I have done my best to check facts and give credit where it is due. In the event that any material is used without proper permission, please contact me so that the oversight can be corrected.

**\*\*COVER IMAGE\*\***

https://www.flickr.com/photos/9750464@N02/49875109173/

**\*\*ADDITIONAL IMAGES\*\***

https://www.flickr.com/photos/watts_photos/31690870574/

https://www.flickr.com/photos/9750464@N02/49875950317/

https://www.flickr.com/photos/watts_photos/22137420196/

https://www.flickr.com/photos/postmanpetecoluk/49620664488/

https://www.flickr.com/photos/9750464@N02/51875483936/

https://www.flickr.com/photos/9750464@N02/51868102144/

https://www.flickr.com/photos/131806380@N05/33171328992/

https://www.flickr.com/photos/smudge9000/51630348537/

https://www.flickr.com/photos/68166820@N08/49368213483/

https://www.flickr.com/photos/guynamedfawkes/51177238435/

Contents

INTRODUCTION ................................................. 9
HABITAT .............................................................. 11
FAMILY ................................................................ 13
APPEARANCE .................................................... 17
BEHAVIOR ........................................................... 19
DIET ...................................................................... 23
SUITABILITY AS PETS ..................................... 27

# INTRODUCTION

The Grey Squirrel is one of the most common creatures that lives with us side-by-side peacefully. It is an animal usually found in many eastern countries; this is why it is called the *Eastern Gray Squirrel* in much of the world.

The tree is the where the grey squirrel builds its home, but you will see them on the ground looking for food and playing.

## HABITAT

The Grey Squirrel is native to southern Canada, as well as eastern and Midwestern America. However, these squirrels can be found anywhere in the eastern countries like India, China, Myanmar, Philippines etc. They are also found from New Brunswick to Manitoba and from the south of Canada to East Texas and into Florida. They are also found in Ireland, Britain, Italy, South Africa, and Australia.

So, as you can see, these beautiful squirrels are at home in many places throughout the world. Maybe in your own backyard!

## FAMILY

The nest of the grey squirrel is called *drey*. They build their home on branchy trees, making them from dry leaves and twigs. When you see a squirrel, it might be gathering acorns – or it might be gathering twigs and leaves to build a nest!

The mating of this squirrel is very private, yet strange at the same time. The female allows the male partner for only a little while in her home. Otherwise, they tend to live alone.

But sometimes, during the winter, she will share hew home with her male companion.

## APPEARANCE

The Grey Squirrel is usually grey with a full, bushy tail. Surprisingly, some of them are more brown than grey.

These squirrels are found in urban areas where people live; they can easily hide in the environment because their color acts as camouflage.

The overall length of the body without tail varies from 9 to 12 inches long and the tail ranges from 7 to 10 inches by itself. The weight of an adult Grey Squirrel varies between 14 and 21 ounces.

## BEHAVIOR

The squirrel family has a very interesting characteristic that is called *scatter-hoarding*. They need to collect all the seeds, nuts and nut pieces which are around near the vicinity of their home. They use these collections as future inventory so that they have it stored up for harsh weather when they cannot get out and look for food easily.

These collections of food are called *caches*. Some of these caches are for temporary storage, but even the short-term caches are close to the squirrel's home where there might be plenty of food around.

Each and every Grey Squirrel is busy making thousands of caches, some of which he (or she) won't ever need to access. Like other animals, they use their sense of smell to find the caches when they are near them.

## DIET

The Eastern Gray Squirrels eat various types of foods, for example, they love the taste of tree bark and tree buds, but some love berries, and different kinds of seeds and acorns.

When there is a scarcity of food in their local territory, they have been known to feast on insects, small frogs, and rodents, but this is somewhat rare. Some squirrels may prey on small birds, eggs of small birds, and their small babies.

Grey Squirrels like all other animals need specific minerals for survival. They will eat bones, antlers, and turtle shells occasionally, because these have this mineral content that suits their physical needs.

These squirrels can cause damage to trees by eating the bark and the soft tissue underneath the branch, which will cause the branch to fall. If they do enough damage, they can even kill a tree by eating away at it!

## SUITABILITY AS PETS

The Eastern Gray Squirrels are considered by some people as good pets. They do get along well with people.

These squirrels will raid bird feeders of seeds of corn, millet, and sometimes sunflower seeds that are meant for the wild birds around your home.

# COLOR ME

# COLOR ME

# COLOR ME

# COLOR ME

# **COLOR ME**

# COLOR ME

# COLOR ME

# COLOR ME

# COLOR ME

# COLOR ME

Please leave me a review here:

*LisaStrattin.com/Review-Vol-62*

**For more Kindle Downloads Visit Lisa Strattin Author Page on Amazon Author Central**

*amazon.com/author/lisastrattin*

To see upcoming titles, visit my website at LisaStrattin.com– most books available on Kindle!

*LisaStrattin.com*

# FREE BOOK

## FOR ALL SUBSCRIBERS – SIGN UP NOW

LisaStrattin.com/Subscribe-Here

LisaStrattin.com/Facebook

LisaStrattin.com/Youtube